The Yorkshire Wolds
IN OLD PHOTOGRAPHS

The Yorkshire Wolds

IN OLD PHOTOGRAPHS

IAN *and* MARGARET SUMNER

Sutton Publishing Limited
Phoenix Mill · Far Thrupp · Stroud
Gloucestershire

First Published 1994

Reprinted in 2002

Copyright © Ian and Margaret Sumner, 1994

British Library Cataloguing in Publication Data.
A catalogue record for this book is available from the British Library.

ISBN 0-7509-3029-2

Typeset in 9/10 Sabon.
Typesetting and origination by
Sutton Publishing Limited.
Printed in Great Britain by
J.H. Haynes & Co. Ltd, Sparkford.

Contents

	Introduction	7
1.	Welton to Market Weighton	9
2.	Hessle to Bishop Burton	35
3.	Goodmanham to Bishop Wilton	45
4.	Cherry Burton to Kirkburn	57
5.	Kirby Grindalythe to Hunmanby	77
6.	Driffield to Sewerby	97
7.	Flamborough Head	123
	Acknowledgements	128

Introduction

The rolling hills of the Yorkshire Wolds stretch in a crescent from Hessle on the Humber around to the towering cliffs of Flamborough Head. To the west lies the Vale of York, to the north the Vale of Pickering, and to the east the Holderness plain. That well-travelled antiquary William Leland, writing in 1586, dismissed them as 'nothing but a heap of mountains'. Perhaps in his day they were nothing much to look at – people had given way to sheep from the fourteenth century onwards, and much land had been allowed to remain uncultivated. Even at the end of the eighteenth century the poet Anna Sewell spoke of 'long tracks of brown and thistly aridity'.

The chalk rocks that lie underneath the thin soils of the Wolds produced the rounded hills, rarely exceeding 600 ft above sea level, cut through with steep-sided valleys where streams only run for two or three months a year. Indeed, it was this very sterility that contributed to the concentration on sheep rearing – almost the whole of the Wolds became a giant sheep run.

The landscape underwent some changes in the early nineteenth century. Sir Christopher Sykes of Sledmere led the way with a large tree-planting scheme to provide shelter belts, and also manured the thin soil to improve the yield. But even when the old communal open-field system gave way to enclosure at around the same time, it made little difference to the number of people in the area, since the fields were replaced by isolated farmsteads among holdings of between 1,500 and 2,000 acres each.

The chalk was not used extensively in building simply because of its softness. In 1794 Isaac Leatham noted that only a few poor buildings were made from chalk, 'mortared' by mud; most were of brick (although some chalk stone cottages lasted until the twentieth century in Flamborough village). Other houses were half-timbered, and thatched roofs were quite common until the nineteenth century. Many field boundaries were marked by turf walls rather than by stone, but these were eventually replaced by hawthorn hedges.

Because the land had been depopulated to make way for sheep, none of the settlements actually on the Wolds grew into anything larger than a big village. Rather, the market centres were towns at the edge of the area, such as Market Weighton, Pocklington and Great Driffield. Kilham, Thwing, Heslerton, Sledmere, Kirkburn, Warter, Lund, North Newbald and South Cave all had a market charter in 1400; but of these, only South Cave and Kilham still had a market of sorts by 1750, the rest decaying with disuse. Upwards of fifty more medieval villages have also disappeared, leaving only a few lumps in the ground and a field name or two to mark their passing.

However, in the eighteenth and nineteenth centuries, man set out to tame nature, and the local gentry strove to manufacture a picturesque setting for their houses and estates. Such houses as those at Boynton, Warter and Sledmere are evidence of this, as are the many merchants' houses crowded into the villages of the south, such as Melton and Welton. Even existing villages were not allowed to stand in the way of progress. The original settlements of Sledmere and Sewerby were demolished and replaced close by to improve the view from the windows of the manor house. Other villages such as North Cliffe, Warter, West Ella and Scampston all suffered to a greater or lesser extent.

This is not to say such improvements were always detrimental. The new houses built to replace the old were often much sounder structurally, and they are to be much admired architecturally. An energetic, improving landlord could thus make a significant contribution to the appearance of the Wolds landscape; none more than Sir Tatton Sykes of Sledmere (1862–1913), who commissioned twelve churches for the villages of his estates, and restored a further eight. One must also mention Lord Hotham, who was responsible for South Dalton church, whose slim noble spire is such a landmark.

Successive agricultural depressions saw a retreat from arable farming on the Wolds and a gradual drift of the population to the towns. The ploughing campaigns of the Second World War brought the former, if not the latter, to a permanent end. Unfortunately the trend towards larger, more economic farms has reduced employment possibilities locally, and although some villages such as Cherry Burton, Walkington, Middleton-on-the-Wolds and Kilham have benefited from the building of new housing estates on their fringes, they serve largely as dormitories for commuters.

Man has wrought great changes on the Wolds. From being 'scarce ought but flints and stones/A few short whins, and strewed with dead sheep's bones', as Edward Anderson wrote in 1792, the area has become among the most fertile and intensively farmed agricultural land in the country. At the same time it is an archaeological site of immense significance, and the chalk grasslands are an important wildlife habitat. It remains an important natural resource for us all.

SECTION ONE

Welton to Market Weighton

The Green Dragon, Welton. It was here that the highwayman Dick Turpin was finally arrested, for horse theft; he was then taken to York, tried and executed. On the right, two men, one in a bath chair, stop for a chat outside the post office.

St Helen's Church at Welton contains some Norman elements, but it was so thoroughly restored by Sir George Gilbert Scott in 1862–3 that it is virtually a new church. The restoration was on behalf of the Harrison-Broadley family, who also donated some Morris glass to the nave and transept windows. The tree which was in full leaf in the previous photo is now totally bare.

Welton Lodge. Welton and its dale was a popular place for a day trip from Hull, and the lodge, part of the Harrison-Broadleys' Welton House estate, offered refreshments for the thirsty traveller.

Welton Grange, here being used as a convalescent home during the First World War. This was another Harrison-Broadley property in the village, previously let to tenants. It was said that it was possible to walk from one end of the riding to the other, and not leave the family's property.

A drag harrow in use on the Wolds above Welton. The harrow was used to break up soil to form a seedbed by dragging the metal frame at an angle across the ploughed ground. The harrow was kept at the correct angle by the series of swing-trees attaching it to the harness.

The house and garden at Brantinghamthorpe. The house was built between 1868 and 1876 for Christopher Sykes, but around an older building. Having nearly bankrupted himself in entertaining the Prince of Wales (later Edward VII) and his set, Sykes was forced to sell it shortly before he died. Sykes himself may be the seated figure here.

Commandeering horses and carts in the Market Place, South Cave, at the outbreak of the First World War. British Army wagons had the horses hitched to a pole, like Wolds wagons, rather than in traces; this tradition lay behind the formation of the Wolds Wagoners in the Sledmere area, in order to provide a ready-made reserve of drivers used to pole wagons.

South Cave Market Place. The road is in fact a diversion off a Roman road which ran from Malton to Brough. The tower of course belongs to the Market Hall, which was built in 1796. Nearer the centre of the picture is The Fox and Coney. The building dates from 1739; a landlord of the eighteenth century, William Goodlad, also carried on the trade of furrier, which perhaps explains the origin of the pub's name.

Commandeering motor vehicles outside the Market Hall. Although the shot is rather distant, from their uniform these could be men of the East Riding Yeomanry. It must still have been quite rare to see so many cars together in the same place. Two of the soldiers are taking advantage of the opportunity to have a good look inside the vehicles.

Bill Smith and his son Bob with their cart outside Suddaby's grocer's shop and The Three Tuns in South Cave Market Place. The pub had been in existence since at least 1752, and here has been recommended by the Cyclists' Touring Club, whose sign is displayed on the wall. It was, however, demolished to make way for a Co-op shop which opened in 1926, moving from the former Suddaby's shop next door.

The proclamation of King George V on the steps of the Market Hall, 1911. A troop of Scouts keeps the crowds back while the proclamation is read out.

The original Cave Castle had been built by 1525, but it was rebuilt for H.B. Barnard in 1797, and remodelled for him in the Gothic style by Henry Hakewell in 1804. It was much extended by his descendant, Charles Edward Gee Boldero Barnard in 1872–5. The parklands, of some 65 acres, including the castle lily pond, were originally laid out by William Emes in 1787, but were extensively restored and altered in 1872.

Church Hill, South Cave. All Saints Church, like Welton, is more restoration than original, and the more recent elements, dating from the late 1840s and '50s, are the work of J.L. Pearson. On the right of the picture is the castle's West Lodge.

West End is the older part of the village; here we are looking eastwards from the last houses on the road.

An entertainment by the South Cave Gypsy Troupe, 24 February 1911, featuring a 'cast of thousands', including Queen Elizabeth I and Joan of Arc (and a gentleman hamming it up on the right).

A group of servers at South Cave Carnival in 1911. It is not known whether they were servants brought from the big houses or merely helpers.

South Cave Cricket Club undertook a tour of Nottinghamshire in August 1909. They are seen here on Retford pavilion steps.

Beverley Road from the clock tower of the Market Hall. The road disappears between Little and Great Wold Sides. South Cave Beck rises from a spring beside the road, and flows over the ground on the left of the picture.

Two women working in the fields outside South Cave. Their headgear may have been old-fashioned, but it did keep the sun off.

All Saints Church and the school, North Cave. The church is mostly thirteenth century with Norman foundations. There has been a school of some kind in North Cave since 1743. This was a boys' school, supported by grants and endowments, until taken over by the National Society in 1840. It amalgamated with the girls' school in 1934.

Westgate, North Cave, looking westwards towards the Wesleyan chapel on Finkle Street corner. On the right is The Albion Hotel, and beyond that The White Hart, where landlady Mrs Daniel Gray held a corn market every Thursday.

Nordham was probably just another part of North Cave village at one time; the route that the road takes is parallel to Churchgate. Here we are looking from a group of houses known as Belgrave Square eastwards towards Nordham itself.

The Bishop of Hull, the Revd Dr Blunt, conducting an open air service at St Austin's Stone in Drewton Dale, 22 July 1905. St Austin's, or St Augustine's, Stone was supposed to have been the place where St Augustine preached Christianity to the Saxons – but it is very unlikely indeed that he ever came so far north. The congregation was composed of local Sunday School teachers.

Hotham Inn. The landlady, Ellen Sargeson, had taken over from George Sargison. It was built in *c.* 1846 as The Queen's Arms, was then renamed The Hotham Inn, and is now The Hotham Arms.

Amen Lane, Hotham, looking northwards. Behind the wall and the trees are the grounds of Hotham House, and the house in the background on the left was the Manor House.

Hotham Hall (which is actually in North Cave parish) was built for the Metham family in 1683, and was extended in the eighteenth century. It was the home of John Stracey-Clitherow.

Colonel John Stracey-Clitherow (1853–1921) was a military man. Having served in the Scots Guards and participated in the Jameson raid in South Africa, he had risen to become Colonel of the East Riding Yeomanry. He became Master of the Holderness Hunt in 1927. He is the man seen standing here; the location of the photo is not known – it may be the grounds of Neswick Hall.

A pause for refreshment while threshing in a Hotham farm stackyard. The men are standing in front of the threshing machine, which is powered by the portable steam engine on the left.

The rededication of St Oswald's Church, Hotham in 1905, after its restoration by F.S. Broderick on behalf of Stracey-Clitherow.

Houses on the road between North and South Newbald.

A view from the tower of North Newbald church, looking north-west down Galegate; the Mires and Ratten Row are both hidden by the houses in the foreground. The low white building at the crossroads was once a smithy.

Another view from the church tower extending the panorama eastwards. The ivy-clad building in the foreground is the Manor House. The long building in the left background is the school and post office, built in 1846. The road disappears over Woodgate Hill, with Cow Dale and Hunger Hill to the right.

A third view from the church tower, this time looking northwards. Behind the trees is the site of Newbald Hall. It formed part of the estate built up by John Clough (d. 1786) and his son, J.W. Clough (d. 1842), but when the estate was sold off it passed to William Henry Harrison-Broadley of Welton, who had it demolished in *c.* 1887. The Primitive Methodist chapel in the foreground was built in 1878, and services were held there until 1956, when it became a store. It was eventually demolished in 1987. The white building facing The Green is The Tiger Inn.

St Nicholas's Church, according to the architectural writer Nikolaus Pevsner, is 'the most complete Norman church in the Riding'. It was apparently built by one Sigarius, who was vicar from 1120. It appears to have missed the ruinous attentions of nineteenth-century restorers, although the roof line of the west end has obviously been altered at some time.

A scene on the Mires looking eastwards near the corner of Galegate (off to the left) and Ratten Row (off to the right). The smithy appears to be doing good business, with three carts and some farm machinery standing outside waiting for the attention of smith George Levitt.

A pump erected on The Green to commemorate the coronation of King Edward VII in 1902. Behind can be seen both of the village's pubs, The Tiger Inn and The New Hotel (only recently renamed The Gnu; the reason for the change is obscure – brewer's whimsy, perhaps). The pump no longer exists, but its site is marked by a small stone.

A view looking up Galegate, North Newbald.

Some children being treated to a donkey ride, outside a row of cottages named Harlands West Villas, which were built in 1835.

Looking towards Sancton church from Gowley Hill, between Low Street and Ratten Row. Just visible on the right is the belfry of the village school.

All Saints Church, Sancton. What makes this church unique in the Riding is the octagonal west tower – the nearest similar example is at Coxwold in the North Riding. The church was rebuilt in 1869–71, and it seems maintenance work is being carried out in this picture.

Sancton Grange Farm, just north of the village. It was built by the lord of the manor, John Broadley of Hull, about 1823–33. Around the time of the photograph the farmer was George Thomas Beal.

High Street, Market Weighton, with The King's Arms, once The Foundry Arms, on the left. Just up the street on the same side is the arch-nemesis of any pub, the Temperance Hall. Both have since been demolished to make way for the buildings at Massey's Corner.

The High Street, a little further up. There are several interesting items in this shot – the *trompe-l'œil* painted brickwork on the wall of Bates Wadworth's painter and decorator's shop on the left; the Registry for servants on the corner of Finkle Street; and in the background The Alma pub on the Market Place, now demolished.

A view towards the end of Southgate. The houses on both sides of the road have since been demolished, those on the right to make way for Princess Road.

Outside the shop of T.G. Lyon & Son, the Central Stores, in the Market Place.

Around the back of Lyon's shop, with carriers taking delivery of dry goods to distribute among the villages. Note the Lyon's delivery boy and his bicycle on the right.

The M.W. Wheelers, with a wide variety of machines, including some with racy drop-handlebars. One man (sitting at the right of the front row) even carries a bugle!

At the railway station awaiting the departure of King Edward VII, who had been visiting Londesborough Park. Drawn up on the left, almost out of the picture, is a group of the East Riding Yeomanry, and the mounted man in the centre of the picture is their major, John Stracey-Clitherow of Hotham Hall.

SECTION TWO
Hessle to Bishop Burton

Little Switzerland, Hessle. The Wolds meet the Humber at Hessle, and the wooded paths were, and are still, a popular place for a walk to get away from it all.

Chalk quarry, Hessle. The chalk was used in the building trades for the production of whiting (an ingredient of putty), and later for the manufacture of cement.

Tranby Croft was built in 1874 for Arthur Wilson MP, a member of the Wilson shipping line family, and is now a girls' school. It was here that the notorious Baccarat Scandal took place, which involved cheating at cards; the Prince of Wales (later Edward VII) was called as a witness in the succeeding court case.

Taking it easy at Tranby Lodge. The house was built around 1810 by Samuel Cooper, a Hull merchant. The building was allowed to fall into decay by the owners in the 1960s, to evade their responsibilities in maintaining such an old building. The remains were finally demolished in 1986.

The centre of Westella – a 'pretty spot', according to the sender of this postcard. The village pond is in the centre, and the buildings on the right are those of Manor House Farm, built in the early nineteenth century, and then 'Gothicized' with the addition of decorative bargeboards and mullioned windows around 1830 by the lords of the manor, the Sykes family.

Another view from a church tower, this time in Kirkella, looking north-westwards along Packman Lane. The fields in the background have now all been built upon. Behind the trees to the left are the grounds of Kirkella Hall, now Hull Golf Club. The large house in the centre is Weston Villa; the yard in the foreground belongs to The Wheatsheaf.

St Peter's Church, Rowley. It was the incumbent of this church, Ezekiel Rogers, who led his dissenting flock to the United States in 1638, leaving the village virtually deserted. Now only the church and the rectory stand on the site.

Taking some horses through Little Weighton village past the pond, which is just out of the picture to the right. The road in the centre goes to Low and White House Farms, the one to the right towards Cottingham.

Looking westwards down Main Street, Skidby. At one time there were two or three pubs in the village, but this was eventually reduced to one, known from at least 1825 as The Half Moon.

Skidby Manor. A manor house had existed in Skidby since at least 1325. Although the original had been rebuilt in the mid-eighteenth century by Ellerker Bradshaw of Risby, it was demolished in the late nineteenth century and replaced by this building.

Walkington Club feast in 1905. The feast was organized by Court Walkington of the Free and Independent Foresters, some of whose officals can be seen wearing sashes in this photograph. Friendly Societies, such as the Foresters and Oddfellows, played an important part in village life by providing a form of health insurance before the introduction of the Welfare State.

Transport old and new outside The Dog and Duck. The landlord at the time, Edward Spence, also farmed at Park Farm. The cart on the left belongs to Hindle's, mineral water manufacturers of Jalland Street, Hull, and presumably has just been making a delivery at the pub.

A horse-drawn Massey Harris reaper and binder in action in the 1930s. The machine cut and bound the sheaves (on the left), which lay on the ground until they could be gathered and stooked before being carted home. Such machines were rare before 1914.

An undated group of Walkington children. Whatever the occasion, perhaps a feast, they are in their Sunday best and all (well, almost all) smiling.

A view familiar to many – Bishop Burton pond and The Altisidora pub in the background. The pub was known as The Evander until 1825, then changed its name to The Horse and Jockey, and again to The Altisidora in 1875, in commemoration of the St Leger winner of 1813, bred locally by Squire Watt. The man on the right is a policeman.

The old Baptist chapel (centre building) on Callas. It was built in 1770 but was demolished because of falling attendances in 1955.

Ploughing near Bishop Burton in the 1930s.

SECTION THREE

Goodmanham to Bishop Wilton

Going for a stroll in the country at Goodmanham. This is on the west side of the village, going towards Market Weighton; the lodge of the Rectory estate is just behind the trees. The man on the left is taking no chances and is carrying an umbrella.

All Saints Church, Goodmanham. The church is mostly Norman; inside is an elaborate font with the inscription 'With owt baptysm no soull ma be saved'. The church was built on the site of a pagan temple, and the village itself was the capital of the Anglian kingdom of Deira.

King Edward VII at Londesborough, October 1905. He was a frequent visitor to Londesborough both before and after his coronation. On this occasion he had arrived on the 23rd for four days' shooting, in a small party which included the Austrian Ambassador, a marquess, two earls and nearly a dozen others, including his mistress, Mrs Keppel. This picture may have been taken either at Goodmanham or near Enthorpe, where the party were riding; the man on the right is probably Major-General Sir Stanley Clarke, another member of the royal party.

Londesborough Park. The original Londesborough Hall had been demolished in 1819 by its owner the Duke of Devonshire and much of the stone is supposed to have gone into the building of an extension to Chatsworth. The land was bought in 1845 by George Hudson, the railway king, who went bankrupt soon afterwards. The earliest part of this house was built in 1839 as a shooting box. It was extended by its new owners, the Londesboroughs, in 1875.

The grounds of Londesborough Park remained little changed from the days of the old hall. The earls of Londesborough continued to improve them in an attempt to compete with the estates of older-established families such as the Sykes.

Crossing the bridge over Burnby Beck in Nunburnholme. The small building on the other side is the smithy.

Cottages at the north end of Town Street in Nunburnholme. They have since been demolished.

The funeral of Lord Nunburnholme on 31 October 1907. The coffin is here being borne by men of the Wilson Line (which he had founded) through torrential rain, from Warter Priory to the edge of the estate, where it was placed on a drag and taken to the church where the burial was to take place.

George Street, Pocklington. On the right is the police court and station, built in 1899–1900, while on the left, on the corner of Kirkland Street, is The Royal Oak (no longer a pub, although the building is still there, much modified).

Two kinds of transport on George Street. Todd's sweet and toy shop on Tute Hill has now been demolished.

Regent Street looking towards the Market Place. The pub on the left is The Old Red Lion.

Railway Street in the snow looking towards the Market Place. On the right is the post office, and in the centre the side of Meynell's grocer's shop can be seen.

Pocklington School. The school was founded in 1514 by John Dolman, Archdeacon of Suffolk, a man from an old Pocklington family. Most of the school's buildings date from a rebuilding in 1850–1.

West Green. The railway level-crossing and the station are hidden by the trees. On the left is the school.

Pocklington from Chapel Hill. The large building on the edge of town is Lyndhurst, owned by the auctioneer Richard Massey English. St Helen's Gate is hidden by the houses, but Percy Street can just be seen on the left. Further on the left, behind the trees at the edge of the photo, is the reservoir of the Pocklington Water Company.

The organizers of a bazaar in aid of the Wesleyan Methodist chapel, some time in the first ten years of this century. The chapel, on Chapmangate, was at one time a barn. Rebuilt several times during the nineteenth century, it is still in use today.

A men-only outing, en route to Millington Pastures in 1913.

A scene in Millington main street looking south-west past The Gate Inn on the right. Note the woman standing with buckets in her hands – there was a spring in the gap between the houses on the left. The trees in the background mark the vicarage grounds.

The corner of Church Street and Silver Street, Huggate. Behind the trees is the smithy, and in the background, behind some more trees, is the church spire. Something must be happening off to the right by the way everyone is looking in that direction.

Huggate again, and the corner of Stock Hill and Beverley Lane. On the left is the Wesleyan chapel, built in 1885 and closed in 1974, and in the background, The Wolds Inn.

The most distinctive feature of Bishop Wilton is its unusually wide green, cut through by the beck. Here we are looking down the village, from just in front of the site of the palace of Archbishop Neville of York, which gave the village its name. Visible on the left is The Fleece Inn, on the corner of Pocklington Lane.

A street scene in Bishop Wilton with a wagon belonging to W. Culine's Steam Circus. In the background is St Edith's Church. The church was restored in 1858–9 by J.L. Pearson for Sir Tatton Sykes of Sledmere around a fourteenth-century core at a cost of between two and four thousand pounds. Parts of the chancel and nave roof were covered in 8,000 gold leaves.

SECTION FOUR
Cherry Burton to Kirkburn

Cherry Burton Hall and behind it the church. The hall was bought by David Fowler, the lord of the manor in 1794, and remained in the family until 1945. The church was built in 1852, to replace a dilapidated smaller structure on the same site.

Workers' cottages, High Gardham farm, 1906. High Gardham farm was built by 1852, as part of the Hotham estate, but was sold off about 1921. When this photograph was taken, the farmer was John Wood, although this was the house where the sender of the postcard, John Drummond, lived.

Church Farm, Etton. In the background are two extremely well crafted 'pikes' or round hay stacks; the man responsible, Joe Allen, took a justifiable pride in his work, even to the extent of going to the Cherry Burton road to look back and check the pikes' symmetry.

Etton church and churchyard in the 1880s. The church was built in 1848–9 in this neo-Norman style, incorporating some medieval elements.

South Dalton church under construction in 1861. The identity of the men in the foreground is unknown, although it is not inconceivable that one is the architect, John Pearson; one might even be Lord Hotham himself. On the left are the remains of the old church, in the process of demolition.

The finished church. Its most notable feature is its slender spire, some 200 ft high, which can be seen for miles around.

The dedication of the lychgate at the church in November 1910. The gates were built by subscriptions from the villagers as a memorial to John, 5th Baron Hotham, who had died in 1907. The gate was designed by Geoffrey Warburton, the agent of the 6th baron, and erected by estate joiners, with additional carvings by Elwell's of Beverley. The 6th baron can be seen here, in front of the gate, with a hand to his ear; within the gate is the Archbishop of York, who conducted the service of dedication, assisted by many of the local clergy.

Another view of the thatched house on the previous page. On the left is the post office, which has replaced the building seen in that photograph.

Dalton Hall, the home of Lord Hotham. The core of the building was built in the 1730s, but the hall was much enlarged in the 1770s and again in 1784.

Front Street, Lockington, at the very western end of the village. In the foreground is Bryan Mills Beck; the junction with Pit Lane is just visible in the background.

Scene in Lockington, with The Rockingham Arms on the right. Although the Marquess of Rockingham, a prominent eighteenth-century politician, was Lord Lieutenant of the East Riding for a time, the inn sign shows that the pub was named after Rockingham, the St Leger winner of 1833, who like Altisidora, was owned by Squire Watt of Bishop Burton.

A seed press in action in the fields around Lockington. At the reins is Yengo Benson, a Beverley man, and a well-known local boxer.

A view westwards across the green at Lund. On the right-hand side is the cross, and behind that, the Wellington Inn. On the left is the post office, with a postman standing in front.

Another view across the green, this time looking southwards. The thatched house, already looking rather dilapidated, has now gone.

Lund club feast in 1909, organized by the St Peter Lodge of the Independent Order of Oddfellows, Manchester Unity, No. 1184.

St Andrew's Church, Middleton-on-the-Wolds. This retains some medieval features but is mostly the work of J.M. Teale of Doncaster; it was completed in 1873–4.

A group of children outside the school house. It was built in 1872 to house no less than 178 children; the population of the whole village in 1901 was only 634. The master was Mr Oliver Ridley, and he was assisted by Miss Harrison and Mrs Carter. The building is no longer used as a school; the front part, the master's house, is still a house, but the back part, the actual school, became a builder's yard.

A scene at East End, with the church just out of the picture to the right. On the right-hand side is the post office, with an enamel advertisement on the wall for Mazawattee Tea. Note that one of the cottages in the background has had a second storey added – the old roof line is just visible with the 'tumbled' bricks of the gable end.

A Foresters' procession, 20 August 1908. The members of the society (the Middleton Foresters Friendly Society) carry their crimson and green banner at the head of the procession.

This house, Watton Abbey, formerly belonged to the prior of the Gilbertine priory founded in 1150. The older parts here date from the fourteenth and fifteenth centuries, but the house was much rebuilt, particularly in the nineteenth century. It was the home of the Coulson family.

Sitting in this smart little trap are Dulcie, Tom and Charlie, the children of Charles Turner, a farmer of Southfield House, North Dalton. The picture is taken in the yard of the farm.

The pond on Cranswick Green. On the right-hand edge of the picture is the school, built in 1875 (although there had been a school of sorts in Cranswick since at least 1743).

A group of boys from the school in 1889, with their teacher George Rayner. These can only be some of the children, since the school had capacity for 160 boys at this time.

The Foresters' Hall in Cranswick, further down Main Street from the previous photograph. The hall was built in 1901 for what was then an independent society, but which later rejoined the Ancient Order of Foresters in 1905 as Court Hotham No. 719. It had 341 members in 1910. An annual concert and dance took place in the hall on 1 January. To the right of the hall is The Pack Horse Inn.

The Revd Wheatley and a group of villagers watch a carriage with liveried servants drive by. It is not possible to see who is in the carriage – the Earl of Londesborough was the lord of the manor, and Frederick Reynard of Sunderlandwick Hall also had land in the parish. The church and vicarage were in Hutton, but all the other amenities were in Cranswick. Hutton people used to say that, apart from going to the church, 'Cransickers' never ventured that far north.

Hutton Cranswick station. The Hull–Bridlington line was opened in 1846, one of 'Railway King' George Hudson's ventures.

Bainton church from the south-west corner of the village. St Andrew's was built, or rather rebuilt, in the middle of the fourteenth century. On the left is a row of houses then called Hudson's Terrace (now merely Hudson Terrace); on the right is the smithy and behind that, in the trees, the outbuildings of the rectory.

A view down Main Street, Bainton. The school is behind the trees on the right.

Bainton House, owned at the time this photograph was taken by Mrs Topham.

A meeting of the Holderness Hunt at Neswick Hall. The hall, which is just visible to the right, was built in the eighteenth century and enlarged in the nineteenth, but was demolished in 1954. It was owned by the Wrangham family.

A railway bridge under construction near Neswick, part of the Driffield–Market Weighton line which opened in 1890. The railways were an important element in the Wolds' economy, giving the farms a much larger market for their produce than just the local town.

The wreck of a Handley Page Harrow aircraft belonging to 75 Squadron, which crashed in a field near Tibthorpe while trying to land at Driffield airfield on the night of 5 April 1938. The crew of five – Sgt. Edward Merchant (pilot), Sgt. Donald Marshall, Cpl. Walter Greaves, LAC Geoffrey Humpherys and AC Ronald Fish (a local man, from Norton) – were all killed. The Harrow was an ungainly, heavy bomber, and would have been an easy target for modern fighters. It was soon relegated to a transport role.

Tibthorpe pump on Well Lane. It was horse drawn at one time, but if no horse was available you had to make your own arrangements, as these four ladies appear to be doing!

The Queen's Head (landlord Robert Leaper), Kirkburn. The sign advertises Russell's Ales, a Malton brewery which was taken over by Melbourne Breweries of Leeds in 1958. For reasons unknown, the man on the left standing outside appears to be wearing his coat tied with a white sash. From the tone of the message on the back of this postcard of 1902, both men may be friends or relations of the Leaper family.

SECTION FIVE
Kirby Grindalythe to Hunmanby

St Andrew's Church, Kirby Grindalythe, built in 1878 by the prominent church restorer G.E. Street for Sir Tatton Sykes, incorporating some medieval elements.

The Cross Keys Inn, Thixendale, at the east end of the village; it has occupied this site since at least 1851. The landlord when this photograph was taken was Herbert Williamson. He had taken over in 1906 from John Towse, whose family still lived in Jewison's Row (the row of cottages on the left of the pub), and one of whose children can be seen standing at their front door.

New Row, Duggleby, c. 1906. The building at the far end was at one time the post office.

Wharram-le-Street church. It is mostly Norman, but with heavy Saxon influences. Wharram is most famous for the nearby deserted village of Wharram Percy.

Looking across towards Acklam from Toft Hill. In the background is the church tower, and behind that Thrussendale Road leading off over Acklam Wold.

A street scene in Burythorpe. Burythorpe was a small parish, with only 227 people in 1891; but it boasted a church, two chapels and a school for fifty pupils.

The post office (left) and the smithy at the north-west corner of Kirby Underdale. At this time the road shown here petered out into a green lane, which divided into two, one fork leading up Howe Hill and the other towards Waterloo Farm.

Sledmere House. Richard Sykes began construction in 1751, but it was completed in this noble restrained style by his descendant Sir Christopher in 1781–8.

Sledmere village, with The Triton Inn on the right. The Triton, an old coaching inn, dates from the second half of the eighteenth century. The houses on the left, however, including the post office, estate office and clerk's house, were all built in the 1890s by John Birch for Sir Tatton Sykes.

The Wolds Wagoners' Memorial, erected in 1919 as a memorial to the Wolds Wagoners' Special Reserve, raised by Sir Mark Sykes before the First World War. The carvings, by Carlo Magnioni to Sir Mark's designs, depict soldiers going off to war.

The funeral of Sir Tatton Sykes on 9 May 1913 at Sledmere church. In the foreground is his son Sir Mark (who was to live only another six years), his wife Edith, and three of their children (left to right) Freya, Richard and Christopher.

The gamekeeper of the Sledmere estate with his family, standing outside his cottage.

A horselad on the Sledmere estate with two of his charges. He is dressed in the standard garb for his job, with a double-breasted waistcoat and bell-bottomed corduroy trousers. The horse on the right has a saddle; the wagoner often rode the nearside horse, particularly when three horses were hitched to the wagon.

The Eleanor cross. This is a copy of a cross first erected in Northamptonshire in 1291. It was erected on the west side of Sledmere by Sir Mark Sykes in 1895, and the work was carried out by Temple Moore. The original crosses marked the stopping points of the funeral procession of King Edward I's queen, on the way to her burial.

North Grimston Vicarage, occupied at this time by the Revd Charles Hall.

Settrington House, which is at the south end of the village. This was built *c.* 1790 for Lord Middleton. The centre was gutted by a fire in 1963, and has been restored to a slightly different appearance.

Settrington, at the bridge where Town Street crosses Settrington Beck, and, in the distance, the junction with Church Lane.

A view of houses on Back Lane along Settrington Beck.

View from Rillington church tower looking down Westgate, the road to Malton. The building in the foreground is The Fleece.

Looking down Rillington High Street from the south end of the village. Behind the trees to the left are the vicarage and the church, whose spire is just visible. The building with the decorated shutters on the right is The Gate pub.

Looking northwards along the main street, Thorpe Bassett. Just out of the picture to the left is the school, while to the right is the chapel, with the tiny smithy building just to its left.

The rector of Cowlam, the Revd James Oliver, in front of his rectory. Much of the site of Cowlam is a deserted medieval village; the rector's flock was drawn from only a few farms.

Foxholes Rectory. Built in the seventeenth century, it was rebuilt *c.* 1716, and the upper storeys added by 1819. The rector at this time was the Revd William Roberts, who was also vicar of Butterwick. The rectory was sold in 1946, and is now called Foxholes Manor.

The pond and Manor Farm, Foxholes. The rectory grounds are just around the bend in the road.

A view of Sherburn taken from the church tower, looking south. The thatched cottage on the right is on the corner of what is now Vicarage Lane. In the left background is the stackyard of Elm Tree Farm, while in the distance on the right are the buildings of Kirk's East Riding Brewery, which was sold off in 1922 to Walker's of York.

On the same day in 1910 that floods hit Driffield, a similar cloudburst affected East Heslerton. The power of the flash flood can be seen in the destruction wrought on this hillside on farmer John Coverdale's Grange Farm.

Fordon, like Cowlam, is a very small settlement indeed, and virtually all of the hamlet can be seen in this photograph, with Low Fordon Farm on the left, and the church on the right. The parish had a population of just thirty-eight in 1901.

Wold Newton Mere and, in the background, The Anvil Arms. The pub had once been The Plough, but had changed to The Blacksmith's Arms by 1867. It surely cannot be a coincidence that the landlady at this time, Mrs Harriet Haw, also carried on the trade of blacksmith from the rear of the pub. Note that the buildings on the left are made from chalk stone rather than bricks.

Thwing. The building on the left is that of Robert Hoggard, tailor. Business must be a little slack, if he is the figure repairing his bicycle.

The Hunmanby/Kilham Road junction, Burton Fleming taken from Butcher's Lane, with The Star Inn on the left. The stream on the right is the Gipsey Race, which flows into the sea at Bridlington.

Front Street in Burton Fleming, looking towards the church. One of the buildings on the right is now the post office.

St Cuthbert's Church, Burton Fleming. It is basically medieval but, as can be seen, much restoration work has been carried out, not always very sympathetically. Burton Fleming was so called after the lords of the manor, the Gant family who, as their name suggests, were from Ghent in Flanders.

South Street, Burton Fleming, just down the road from the Butcher's Lane photograph (on p. 93). On the right is the shop of Joseph Potter, tailor and draper. It is a comment on the self-sufficiency of many villages, like Burton Fleming and Thwing, that they could support a tailor's business. In the background is The Buck Inn.

Hunmanby, and although the postcard says 'Station Road', this was marked on old maps as Bridlington Street. Here you are looking towards the centre of the village, with the buildings of Town Farm on the left.

Hunmanby again. This is the view from the corner of Northgate, coming from the left, and Stonegate. On the right, set back from the road, are the garden walls of the almshouses. These were in existence from at least 1743, and were said to have been set up by a member of the Osbaldeston family. They had almost totally disappeared by 1970.

SECTION SIX
Driffield to Sewerby

Driving sheep down Beverley Road, Driffield, *c.* 1912. This is not something that could be recommended these days.

Driffield station yard. Several carriages and an early bus wait for the arrival of a train. At one time The Bell Hotel had a special carriage, 'The Bell Bus', which used to meet travellers off the train and take them straight to the hotel. The motor bus services were operated by the North Eastern Railway. The railway line between Hull and Bridlington was opened in 1846; this was joined by another to Malton in 1854, and one to Market Weighton in 1890.

Middle Street South, looking towards the Market Place. Dunns has a prominent display of boots hanging outside its windows; the sign over the door and the one in the street make sure you know where the shop is and what it sells.

Driffield Market Place in the late afternoon, with the market closing down for the day, although there are still a lot of people about. In the foreground, by the lamppost, is a horse-drawn grass cutter. The attraction of the market is obvious from the number of hotels here: The Bell on the left; The Keys on the right; Honor's Temperance Hotel almost in the centre of the picture; and The Falcon in the distance.

The founder of the booksellers of Middle Street, John Sokell. He was an enthusiastic cyclist, and won several races in the 1880s on the machine pictured here.

Looking down Middle Street North from the Market Place. Yet another hotel, The Swan, is on the right-hand side. Note the impressive dundreary whiskers of one of the men on the left.

Mill Street, looking towards the Church of England school in the background. No doubt the customers of The Full Measure Tavern on the right insisted on just that! The road led to the King's Mill.

A quiet day on Middle Street during the 1920s. On the face of it this is a rather timeless photograph, but the march of progress is revealed on the left-hand side of the road, where there is a garage, complete with petrol pump.

The corner of Eastgate North, looking back towards the town, near Windmill Hill.

All Saints, Driffield. Built mostly in the early thirteenth century, the 110 ft tower is a prominent local landmark.

The corner of Eastgate South and New Road. The proprietor of the shop on the right, Mr Beesley, was obviously a great believer in the power of advertising, with enamel signs for Fry's and Rowntree's chocolate, Sunlight soap, Colman's mustard, Quaker Oats, Bryant and May matches and Watson's 'matchless cleaner'.

River Head. The Driffield Canal, which linked the town to the navigable part of the River Hull, was opened in 1772. The crane shown in both of these pictures had a lifting capacity of 3 tons. Oilcake and flour were the main products sent out of the town via the canal, while coal, linseed and other dry goods were brought in. The large chimney in the background is that of Hanson's Mill, which was demolished c. 1900.

The results of the floods of 1910 near the Cattle Market, Galloway Street. The pens and the market manager's office can be seen in the background. A cloudburst at Cowlam on 20 May 1910 sent a flash flood down a dry valley and thus into Driffield Beck. The beck could not cope with the sudden rush of water and overflowed into Exchange Street and Eastgate.

The Rose and Crown, River Head, during the floods.

Repairing flood damage again, this time with interested spectators. The phrase 'I love work – I could watch it all day' perhaps springs to mind.

The floods at River Head. On the left is The Blue Bell pub.

The Blue Bell, River Head. It was a previous landlord of The Blue Bell, William Porter, who had been responsible for the building of the Driffield Canal. The canal brought prosperity to Driffield, but sounded the death knell for Kilham's prosperity as a market centre.

The Primitive Methodist chapel was built in 1875, and had seats for 1,000 people. Driffield had a particularly strong nonconformist tradition – Wesley himself had preached in the Market Place in 1772.

The Poor Law Institution, on Bridlington Road, built in 1866 and only recently demolished.

A prizewinning team from D Company, 2nd Volunteer Battalion, East Yorkshire Regiment in 1906. D Company was recruited in the Driffield area, and had won the competition in the previous year as well. The Bingham Trophy, for the Yorkshire Scouting and Skirmishing Competition, contained 1,000 ounces of silver, but was melted down during the First World War.

The destruction of the King's Mill by fire in 1906. The King's Mill was to the west of the town, near Little Driffield. It had already seen a disastrous fire in 1887, most probably the result of a dust explosion, when the building was completely razed to the ground. Rebuilt soon afterwards, it was struck by catastrophe a second time.

A rural scene at Little Driffield, looking towards the church. The view is taken from the south or south-east, looking across Little Driffield Beck.

The Old Hall, Elmswell. It was built in 1634 by Henry Best, the author of *The Farming Book*, an invaluable account of seventeenth-century agriculture.

Thatched cottages at Elmswell. Sadly the name of this gentleman is not known, nor the exact location of the cottages. A dormer window has been put in, but the roof in front of it is slated rather than thatched.

Pulham, Wetwang, looking towards the junction with the Tibthorpe road. At one time this was the main road into the village, but it has since been bypassed.

Wetwang again, this time looking across The Mere at The Black Swan and the corner of Northfield Well Road.

The post mill, Wetwang. It was situated in the north-west corner of the village, on Northfield Road. Post mills, in which the whole structure turned around a central post, were becoming old-fashioned by the middle of the nineteenth century, and were being replaced by tower mills, in which only the top of the mill, the cap, revolved with the sails.

Looking westwards on the York road in Wetwang; the post office is in the foreground, and behind that, The Rose and Crown.

A row of cottages on the south side of Fimber village on the York road. The building on the right is the Wesleyan chapel.

Fridaythorpe Club feast 28 June 1907, probably organized by the Heart and Hand Lodge of the Oddfellows, Manchester Unity, No. 8272, which was certainly active in the village from 1908.

A view across the more westerly of the two ponds in Fridaythorpe.

'Front Street', Langtoft. This is actually Main Street, looking southwards towards the junction with Back Street.

The Rudston Monolith. This is the largest standing stone in Britain, some 25½ ft tall and 6 ft wide. It is gritstone, and the nearest outcrop of that particular rock is at Cayton Bay, some 10 miles away.

A decorated Kilham farm wagon taking women and children on a day out, probably to Bridlington. They would leave at about six o'clock in the morning, and not get back until nine. Wagoners and farmers took great pride in the turn out of horses and wagons on these occasions, as it reflected on their own reputation. Here, the horses appear to be a matched pair of greys, and are elaborately decorated, with brasses on their collars. The sign on the building behind is that of Tom Frost's butcher's shop.

A second farm wagon, this time belonging to Joseph Wilson, who has his name painted on its side. Wilson's horses have flowers around the headband, forehead and nose bands, as well as on the hames of the collar, and ribbon around their neck and britchings.

Looking eastwards along Church Street, Kilham, by Baptist Street corner, just visible on the right. The cottages in the next photograph are just visible in the background, and probably face into what was the Market Place. On the right is the grocer's shop of Beck and Sons, The Star (landlady Miss Jane Morgantroy) and the post office.

All Saints Church, Kilham, from the south-east. It contains much Norman work, particularly in the doorway and nave.

The Jacobean gateway of Burton Agnes Hall, with a group of sightseers at the gate, and the village policeman keeping an eye on things from the left.

A landau outside Burton Agnes church. The identities of the passengers are unknown, but the driver may be George Chandler, the village's only carrier.

Sewerby Hall was built *c.* 1714, and was the home of the Greame family. The wings were added in 1808. The surrounding parkland was created in the nineteenth century, by diverting the road to Flamborough as well as demolishing several of the village houses.

Sewerby church, built in 1848 in a neo-Norman style by George Gilbert Scott for Yarburgh Greame. The style marked a departure for Scott, and was due to the constant interference of his employer, who was subject to what Scott referred to as 'fads'.

The scene at the junction of Sewerby Lane and Back Lane.

SECTION SEVEN
Flamborough Head

The scene looking up Church Hill, Reighton; the church tower can just be seen behind the branches of the tree in the centre. On the left is Manor House Farm, while on the right are Rotten Row and St Helen's Lane. The village evolved into two almost separate settlements, one here and the other at the top of the hill, around the church.

Dane's Dyke. A massive earth bank 18 ft high and 2½ miles long, it is probably not Danish at all, but dates from the Bronze Age. The presence of a ditch on the west side would suggest that if it is a defence work, it was to defend the Head from the rest of the Riding, and not the Riding from Vikings.

Cliff climbers at Bempton. Fowling rights were held by the tenants of land adjoining the cliffs, and 'climbers' went down by methods such as this to find eggs for eating and for collectors.

North Landing, Flamborough Head. Always a refuge from the sea, a lifeboat was first stationed here in 1871. A steam winch was later added to help haul boats out of the water, and a concrete slipway built in 1924.

The 'new' lighthouse, built in 1806. Only a stump remains of the tower of the old lighthouse, which was built *c.* 1674. However, it had relied on voluntary contributions, and the money was never available for the lantern to be lit.

Acknowledgements

We would like to thank the following for their help and for the loan of pictures:

East Yorkshire Local History Society • Humberside Leisure Services
the staff of Beverley Local History Library • Martin Craven
Humberside County Record Office • Chris Ketchell
Chris and Philippa Bosworth • Roy Wilson.